THE DISTANT MIRROR TAROT

THE MAJOR ARCANA

DAVID MAJOR

ADISTANTMIRROR.COM

Copyright © 2025 A Distant Mirror

ISBN 978-1-7635683-1-0

The content of this book is taken from the companion book to the *Distant Mirror Tarot* deck. That book is available in both print and ebook formats, and contains descriptions of the full tarot deck, with each card of the four suits being given the same treatment as the major arcana are in this edition.

A DISTANT MIRROR

Email: mail@adistantmirror.com
Web: adistantmirror.com

CONTENTS

INTRODUCTION 4

THE MAJOR ARCANA

    0.   THE FOOL 8

    1.   THE MAGICIAN 12

    2.   THE PRIESTESS 16

    3.   THE EMPRESS 20

    4.   THE EMPEROR 24

    5.   THE POPE 28

    6.   THE LOVERS 32

    7.   THE CHARIOT 36

    8.   JUSTICE 40

    9.   THE HERMIT 44

   10.   THE WHEEL 48

   11.   STRENGTH 52

   12.   THE HANGED MAN 56

   13.   DEATH 60

   14.   TEMPERANCE 64

   15.   THE DEVIL 68

   16.   THE TOWER 72

   17.   THE STAR 76

   18.   THE MOON 80

   19.   THE SUN 84

   20.   JUDGEMENT 88

   21.   THE WORLD 92

THE FOUR SUITS 96

INTRODUCTION

Welcome to the world of *The Distant Mirror Tarot*.

While often seen as a system of fortune-telling, the tarot's true power lies in its illumination of the hidden patterns of our lives, offering wisdom and clarity through the universal language of archetypes.

The tarot's history is a journey of transformation, first appearing in 15th-century Italy, not as a mystical guide, but as a beautifully illustrated card game for the nobility. It was

called *tarocchi*. The tarot's journey since then, however, has been one of profound transformation. For over 300 years after its creation in 15th-century Italy, the deck was not a mystical tool but a prosaic cultural artifact.

For decades, it remained a game of leisure among the rich, with no connection at all to anything occult or mystical. If you look at the earliest tarot images from that time, as found in the Visconti-Sforza decks from the mid-1400s, it is immediately obvious that the images are earthly and grounded in daily life, to the point of being ordinary.

There is no kabbalah, nor is there any astrology or numerology. There is nothing esoteric at all.

The earliest versions of the 'Marseille pattern' were simply common, mass-produced versions of this game, printed roughly on the cheapest possible paper.

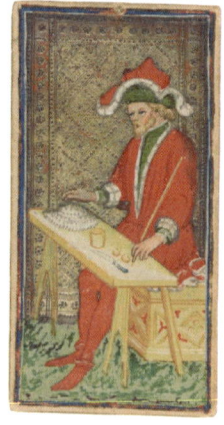 

The great shift occurred in the late 18th century when French occultists 'rediscovered' the tarot, claiming, for the first time, that its images were a hidden book of ancient mystical wisdom and truth.

4 / THE MAJOR ARCANA

This transformation was fundamental. The simple street performer, the Juggler, was reimagined as the Magician, a master of the four elements. The enigmatic Popess, once a mere female pope, became the High Priestess, the guardian of sacred secrets.

Over time, these layers of meaning deepened: the medieval Devil, once a simple boogeyman, was famously linked by 19th-century occultist Eliphas Lévi to Baphomet, and later connected by modern writers to the rebellious Babylonian demoness Lilith, transforming him into a complex symbol of shadow, materialism, and even, in some decks, liberation.

The tarot has indeed moved on from its roots.

The *Distant Mirror Tarot* honors this lineage, serving as a modern reflection of these historical origins, where art and intuition come together and meet the modern world.

At the heart of this tradition are the twenty-two cards you are about to explore: the Major Arcana. These are the great pillars of the tarot, representing the universal milestones and spiritual lessons of life's journey, which tell the story of the soul's passage through the world.

The journey begins with the unnumbered Fool, who takes a leap of faith into the unknown. His path will lead him through encounters with the Magician's raw power, the Priestess's deep intuition, the Emperor's worldly authority, and the Hermit's

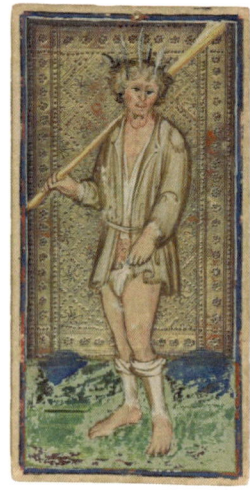  

solitary wisdom.

The journey reaches its end, and a new beginning, with the Judgement and the World.

Each card is a masterpiece of Neo-Classical art, designed not only to be read but to be experienced. You have before you not just a rich collection of Neo-Classically-inspired images, but a profound tool for self-reflection, and a timeless mirror to the soul's equally timeless questions.

How to Read a Simple Spread

You can use these 22 Major Arcana cards on their own for a powerful reading. Because these cards represent life's great themes, they are perfect for exploring the 'big picture' questions.

Shuffle the 22 cards while focusing on your question.

Lay three cards from left to right:

The Root: The core of the situation, or the past lesson that is shaping your present.

The Heart: The central truth of the matter right now; the main challenge or opportunity that faces you.

The Path: The potential outcome or the next great lesson you are moving toward.

Look at the cards as a single story. The journey from Card 1 to Card 3 reveals the spiritual lesson at the heart of your question.

A Glimpse of the Journey

This guide is a special introduction to the Major Arcana – the archetypal soul of the tarot that provides its structure and spiritual depth.

Please know this book is drawn from the comprehensive guidebook that accompanies the complete 78-card *Distant Mirror Tarot* deck. The full book delves deeper, exploring the rich tapestry of the four suits of the Minor Arcana. These fifty-six cards tell the stories of our day-to-day lives, giving voice to the subtle currents that shape our experience. They represent the *how* of our journey, while the Majors represent the *why*.

The complete guidebook explores: the fiery Wands of passion and creation; the deep Cups of the heart, governing our emotions and intuition; the sharp Swords of the intellect, representing our thoughts and conflicts; and the grounded Coins of the material world, speaking to our work and legacy. Together, the Major and Minor Arcana create a complete system for understanding the human experience.

We hope this exploration of the Major Arcana enriches your path and inspires you to continue. The twenty-two cards you are about to meet are the resonant heart of the deck, holding the keys to a deeper understanding of yourself and the world.

May they serve you as a trusted mirror, reflecting the wisdom, courage, and magic that already reside within you.

0. THE FOOL

The beginning and the end of the journey.

Keywords

New beginnings, spontaneity, adventure, innocence, potential, a leap of faith, impetuous, impulse.

Practical guidance

- *Trust the process* and take the first step, even if the outcome is unclear.
- *Balance spontaneity with mindfulness* – embrace adventure, but stay grounded.
- *Be open to wisdom from all sources* – whether people, experiences, or intuition.
- *Remember that mistakes are not failures,* but valuable lessons on the journey.
- *Don't let fear of the unknown stop you.* Life is meant to be lived fully.

> "Follow your inner moonlight; don't hide the madness."
>
> – Allen Ginsberg
>
> Intuition and creativity often defy logic. The Fool encourages us to embrace our unique inner self, even when it doesn't conform to expectations.

Imagery and symbolism

The Fool wears a richly embroidered outfit, adorned with gold filigree, that blends whimsy with regal sophistication. His armored shoulders suggest a traveler who is both bold and prepared for anything.

He carries a spherical, jewel-encrusted bag secured with ornate golden fastenings, its intricate patterns resembling celestial constellations – potential and hidden wisdom. His loyal dog leaps beside him, all instinct and devotion.

The Fool treads a cracked stone path, surrounded by wildflowers and rugged terrain, symbols of life's unpredictability. The towering mountains and swirling clouds foretell the vast scale of his journey.

Hovering before him, leading the way, is a surreal, fox-like creature with an ornate, crown-like headdress. Its mischievous yet knowing gaze suggests it is more than an ordinary animal – it is a trickster-guide, sent to test the Fool's awareness and instincts.

Traditional meaning

The Fool marks the beginning of a journey filled with promise, uncertainty, and adventure.

He is the spirit of exploration, urging one to step into the unknown with trust and enthusiasm.

This card often signals a fresh start or a pivotal moment when instinct and courage must outweigh fear. It encourages a willingness to embrace change, even when the path is unclear.

Each step forward becomes an opportunity for growth, learning, and self-discovery.

The Psychology of Risk

The Fool's journey mirrors the psychological principle that stepping into the unknown fosters self-discovery.

Modern psychology recognizes that risk-taking is essential for growth. Studies suggest that those who embrace uncertainty and learn from failure are more likely to succeed.

The Fool represents this mindset – stepping forward despite fear, learning from mistakes, and evolving through experience.

Neuroscientific studies reveal that risk-taking activates the brain's reward system, reinforcing adaptability. Fear of failure often holds people back, yet those who take calculated risks strengthen their ability to navigate uncertainty – an essential skill in today's world.

Just as The Fool's path is filled with twists and surprises, life's greatest lessons come from the leaps we dare to take.

Modern interpretation

The Fool invites us to explore the delicate balance between the material and the mystical, much like the modern struggle between digital identity and real-world authenticity. His opulent attire and surreal surroundings suggest that new beginnings are not merely external changes, but also internal awakenings – akin to stepping into the unknown of a new technology, career path, or social movement.

The Fool reminds us that in a world increasingly driven by artificial intelligence and rapid innovation, adaptability is just as vital as intuition.

His presence reminds us that curiosity, confidence, and openness to life's surprises are the keys to embracing the unknown, even in an era where uncertainty is a defining feature of progress.

Reversed

Reversed, the Fool warns of recklessness or unpreparedness.

The seeker could be ignoring red flags, rushing headlong into a situation without due consideration, or acting on impulse without weighing the consequences.

Conversely, it can signify hesitancy – is fear holding you back from embracing new opportunities, or trusting in the natural flow of life?

Reversed, the vibrant imagery of the Fool's path now serves as a caution: a leap of faith must still be guided by awareness.

> In quantum physics, the idea that observation changes reality reflects The Fool's dance between belief and experience.

Associations

- *The Wanderer* symbolizes freedom, limitless potential, nonconformity, and the courage to embrace the unknown.
- *Loki*, the trickster of Norse mythology, embodies chaos, transformation, unpredictability, and the disruption of norms.
- *Don Quixote* – the literary adventurer who takes a leap of faith by abandoning his mundane life to pursue an idealistic and seemingly mad quest.
- *The Court Jester*, under the protection of 'foolishness,' could speak profound truths to royalty, and disrupt rigid conventions. This figure represents the nonconformity and hidden wisdom of the Fool.

Final thought

The Fool dares us to embrace life's unpredictability with wonder and courage.

The road ahead may be uneven, the skies uncertain, but the journey itself is the destination.

In stepping forward, we do not abandon reason – we simply choose faith over fear, trusting that the unknown holds as much magic as mystery.

1. THE MAGICIAN

Initiating action and creation.

Keywords

Power, skill, manifestation, resourcefulness, creativity, willpower, mastery, transformation.

Practical guidance

- *Focus on your strengths* and use them.
- *Align your actions with your intentions* to create meaningful results.
- *Trust in your ability to adapt and innovate* when faced with challenges.
- *Avoid overthinking.* Action is key to manifestation.
- *Reflect on your available resources*, both internal and external, and utilize them effectively.

> **Knowledge without action is wasted potential. The Magician teaches us that real mastery comes from merging skill, willpower, and intent into decisive action.**

Imagery and symbolism

The Magician sits confidently at his workbench, surrounded by tools of magic and alchemy. His deep blue robes, lined with red accents, suggest a combination of intellect and passion.

The tools scattered around him – alchemical vessels, ancient parchments, and mystical symbols – represent his mastery over transformation and the fusion of knowledge and action. Hanging lanterns and orbs reinforce his control over light and knowledge, illuminating the path to creation.

Above his left hand he balances a spider, a master weaver of intricate realities. This symbolizes his control over the delicate threads of fate, his patience, and his ability to manifest complex creations from a single point of intention.

His right hand hovers above the table, fingers poised, as if marshaling unseen energies and weaving his will directly into the world.

Above him, a glowing full moon grants intuition and awareness of the cycles of creation, while the aura of another hidden moon shines behind him.

The Magician and the Science of Focus

Focus and intention are crucial for success.

The Magician embodies the concept of deliberate practice – the structured and intentional effort that separates experts from amateurs. Research has shown that mastery is not just about talent, but about repeated, focused effort combined with continuous improvement.

In an age of constant distraction, the Magician's lesson is clear: intentional action, aligned with skill and knowledge, is the key to transformation. Whether in art, business, or personal growth, success requires not just having the tools, but knowing how and when to use them.

Traditional meaning

The Magician represents mastery, resourcefulness, and the power to bring ideas into reality. He signifies a moment of opportunity in which the seeker can take control of his destiny by applying knowledge, confidence, and skill.

This card appears when the time is right to act with determination and trust in one's abilities.

It is a call to use all tools – both material and intellectual – to manifest desires. This card inspires self-confidence, encouraging belief in our power to shape life through focused intention and action.

Modern interpretation

In the modern world, the Magician is the innovator who uses available tools to manifest a unique vision. He is the master of synthesis, applying willpower to existing resources to create something transformative.

A perfect example is Steve Jobs. He famously didn't invent the mouse or the graphical user interface, but like the Magician with the four suits on his table, he combined these existing elements with his relentless creative focus. Through this alchemy of skill and intention, he manifested products that changed our world. This reminds us that we are all architects of our own reality if we use the tools we have with precision and purpose.

Reversed

When reversed, the Magician warns of manipulation, deception, or misuse of power. It might indicate a lack of focus, procrastination, or an inability to recognize available resources. It can serve as a warning to align intentions with integrity, avoiding any trickery or shortcuts that could undermine long-term success.

The Magician reversed can also indicate self-doubt, lack of confidence, or a failure to take action despite having the necessary tools. Here, he reminds us that wasted potential can be just as harmful as misuse of power.

> "Any sufficiently advanced technology is indistinguishable from magic." – Arthur C. Clarke

Associations

- The *archetype of the Creator*, symbolizing manifestation, potential, and mastery.
- *Thoth* – the Egyptian god of wisdom, writing, and magic, embodying intellect and manifestation.
- *The Alchemist* – a figure found in history and legend, embodying the pursuit of transformation and higher knowledge.

> "Those things which we persist in doing become easier – not because the nature of the task has changed, but because our ability to do it has increased." – Ralph Waldo Emerson

Final thought

The Magician reminds us that we are the architects of our lives. By focusing willpower, creativity, and resources, we manifest desires and transform reality.

Trust your abilities – true mastery harmonizes thought, action, and intention. Step into your role with purpose, clarity, and confidence, knowing that the tools for success are within reach.

2. THE PRIESTESS

The guardian of the subconscious and inner realms.

Keywords

Intuition, mystery, wisdom, sacred knowledge, serenity, spiritual insight.

Practical guidance

- *Trust your instincts* and let intuition guide you.
- *Seek wisdom* through reflection and contemplation.
- *Take time to understand* the deeper meaning behind events and emotions.
- *Be open to exploring* spiritual practices or meditative disciplines.
- *Avoid rushing for answers*; allow them to unfold naturally.
- *Protect your energy* and set boundaries.

> "The quieter you become, the more you can hear."
> – Ram Dass

Imagery and symbolism

The Priestess sits in serene contemplation on a stone throne, positioned between two classical pillars that represent the gateway between the conscious and unconscious realms.

Her flowing white robes symbolize purity and wisdom, draping over her and the stone, connecting her physically to her sacred space. A luminous full moon hangs directly behind her head like a halo, signifying the peak of intuitive power, hidden cycles, and the illumination of the inner world.

In her hands she holds an open book, representing sacred knowledge and hidden truths, which she absorbs with a downcast, meditative gaze. A great white veil covers her head and drapes over the pillars on either side, resembling wings and symbolizing the thin barrier between the seen and unseen worlds. The pillars frame her as the guardian of dualities – light and shadow, reason and intuition – reminding us that the deepest truths are found not in the outer world, but by looking within.

Traditional meaning

The Priestess brings intuition, mystery, and hidden wisdom. She is a guide to the inner realms, urging the seeker to trust his instincts and explore the depths of their subconscious.

She often appears when answers are not found externally but reside within. This card encourages patience, reflection, and deep listening to one's inner voice. The Priestess also represents the importance of divine timing – some truths reveal themselves only when we are truly ready to understand them. She reminds us that wisdom cannot be forced but must be received with openness and trust in the natural flow of life.

Modern interpretation

In today's hyper-connected world, the Priestess represents a radical act of stillness. She is a counterbalance to the noise of social media and endless opinions, urging you to disconnect from external validation, and hear the profound wisdom of your own subconscious.

For example, imagine you are offered a job that seems perfect on paper. Logic, data, and the advice of others all point to accepting it. Yet, you have a persistent feeling of unease – a gut instinct that something isn't right. The Priestess advises you to honor this intuitive data as much as any spreadsheet. Her wisdom lies in pausing, stepping back from the pressure to make the 'logical' choice, and trusting that this inner voice holds a truth that surface-level facts cannot reveal.

Reversed

This reversal suggests confusion, withheld secrets, or a disconnect from intuition. It may indicate ignoring inner guidance or being too influenced by external voices. This position calls for a return to self-awareness.

A reversed Priestess may also signify fear of the unknown or resistance to deeper emotional exploration. It reminds us to face these fears with courage and seek clarity through introspection. It also warns against relying too much on others for answers instead of trusting one's inner wisdom.

The Priestess and the Science of Intuition

Modern neuroscience suggests that intuition is not just 'mystical' – it is a cognitive process during which the brain rapidly synthesizes information.

The Priestess represents this ability to perceive beyond logic, encouraging us to trust the deep, instinctual wisdom that operates beneath conscious awareness.

Associations

- *Persephone, Queen of the Underworld.* The Greek goddess of duality and mystery, whose journey between the worlds of light and shadow mirrors the Priestess's access to the wisdom of the subconscious.

- *The Oracle archetype.* A conduit for divine, hidden knowledge. Like the Oracle of Delphi, the Priestess accesses truths that lie beyond logic, revealing insights gained through deep intuition.

> "Your vision will become clear only when you can look into your own heart. Who looks outside, dreams; who looks inside, awakes." – *Carl Jung*

Jung believed that the unconscious mind holds the key to self-discovery. Like the Priestess, who guards the mysteries of the subconscious, Jung's concept of individuation teaches us that true wisdom comes from integrating both our known and hidden selves. When we listen to our intuition, we align with our real self.

Final thought

The Priestess invites you to enter the quiet sanctum of your inner world. She asks you to listen deeply, trust the wisdom within, and honor life's sacred mysteries.

Explore the unknown with grace and serenity, knowing that the answers you seek are already within. By cultivating patience and nurturing your intuition, you can navigate life's complexities with clarity and confidence.

3. THE EMPRESS

The creator and nurturer of life.

Keywords

Abundance, nurturing, creativity, fertility, beauty, harmony.

Practical guidance

- *Embrace creativity* and trust in your ability to bring ideas to life, no matter how small they seem.
- *Nurture relationships and cultivate harmony* in your environment, fostering love, support, and mutual growth.
- *Practice gratitude* for the abundance in your life, recognizing the beauty in everyday moments.
- *Reconnect with nature* for balance and inspiration, allowing its rhythms to guide your own.
- *Prioritize self-care and personal growth*, ensuring that your well-being remains a foundation for others.

Imagery and symbolism

The Empress sits regally on a gilded throne, surrounded by vibrant flowers symbolizing life and abundance. Her flowing blue gown, simple yet elegant, is adorned with layered gold necklaces and jewelry that catch the light, symbolizing her wealth, wisdom, and divine femininity.

Two songbirds flutter near her, celebrating harmony, freedom, and communication. The golden frame of her throne enhances her majesty, while the red cushions and the red of the flowers together suggest her warmth and passion.

The Empress's serene expression conveys wisdom and strength, embodying both gentleness and creative power.

> "Nature does not hurry, yet everything is accomplished."
> – Lao Tzu

Traditional meaning

Creation, nurturing, and abundance. The Empress signals growth and the ability to turn ideas into reality. She encourages finding joy in creativity and caring for others.

She urges appreciation of life's abundance – whether material, emotional, or spiritual. She also calls us to connect with nature and its cycles, embracing renewal and harmony.

Modern interpretation

The Empress encourages us to embrace creativity and nurture ourselves and others. She reminds us to slow down, appreciate beauty, and recognize that creativity can be found in both grand and simple moments. She urges us to find balance in giving and receiving and to reconnect with what is truly important, such as growth, love, and harmony.

The Empress's lesson also includes sustainability and mindful consumption. She calls on us to care for ourselves, our communities, and the world, which fosters balance and abundance. In the modern world, this is reflected in the rise of sustainable living movements, such as organic farming, ethical fashion, and self-care practices that focus on holistic well-being. By prioritizing harmony with nature and conscious creation, a world where people and the environment can thrive is cultivated.

> Creativity is not limited to art – it's in the meals we cook, the words we write, and the moments we shape. The Empress reminds us that every act of creation, no matter how small, contributes to the beauty and harmony of life.

Reversed

A reversed Empress suggests creative blocks, neglect, or overindulgence. It warns against ignoring self-care or overextending in relationships.

This position calls for balance – nurture yourself as much as you nurture others. It may also indicate material excess or a lack of discipline, urging a return to grounding and intention.

Associations

- *The Great Mother* is a recurring figure in mythology and spirituality, embodying the ultimate source of life and protection, creation and abundance, embodying the cycle of life and renewal.
- *Demeter*, the Greek goddess of fertility, agriculture, and the nurturing forces of nature.
- *The Cornucopia* is a universal symbol of prosperity, nourishment, and fertility.
- *Galadriel of Lothlórien*. The elven queen from *The Lord of the Rings* rules over a protected, timeless, and beautiful forest realm. She is a nurturing and powerful feminine figure who offers sanctuary and fosters growth, embodying the Empress's divine and creative grace.

> "Beauty is truth, truth beauty – that is all ye know on earth, and all ye need to know."
> – John Keats

The Empress and the Cycle of Creation

Just as nature moves in cycles – birth, growth, harvest, and rest – so too does creativity. The Empress teaches that creation is not just about producing but allowing ideas to bloom in their own time. Patience and nurturing lead to fulfillment. Like a well-tended garden, life flourishes with attention and care.

As Vincent van Gogh once said, "Great things are not done by impulse, but by a series of small things brought together."

Final thought

The Empress invites you to take on the role of a nurturer and creator. True abundance comes from the care we give, the love we share, and the creativity we express.

By honoring life's cycles, cultivating beauty, embracing growth, and nurturing others, we nurture ourselves, and in creating, we discover our purpose. Through patience and intention, we create a world of abundance and fulfillment.

4. THE EMPEROR

The embodiment of order and foundation.

Keywords

Authority, structure, stability, discipline, leadership, power.

Practical guidance

- *Take charge of your circumstances* by setting clear goals and creating a plan of action.
- *Recognize the importance of structure* in achieving long-term success.
- *Avoid being overly rigid or controlling*; adapt when necessary.
- *Focus on creating a stable foundation* for yourself and those who depend on you.

Imagery and symbolism

The Emperor sits upon a grand throne, its ornate carvings and gold detailing signifying his strength, authority, and dominion over the material world. He wears rich red robes, lined with golden embroidery, representing power, passion, and leadership. A gilded crown rests firmly on his head, marking his role as a ruler and protector.

Behind him, an intricate stained-glass window displays a celestial compass, symbolizing order, balance, and the guiding principles of leadership. At his feet sit golden objects – urns, goblets, and scepters – representing material wealth, wisdom, and the rewards of discipline and control. His piercing gaze reflects wisdom gained through experience, reinforcing his image as a just and resolute leader.

His commanding yet composed posture embodies the balance between strength and stability, while the symmetrical architecture surrounding him emphasizes structure, discipline, and the firm foundations required for stability and growth.

The Emperor and the art of leadership

True leadership is not about control but about guidance and responsibility. Great leaders inspire confidence and provide stability, shaping a foundation where others can thrive. The Emperor reminds us that strength and wisdom must go hand in hand.

Traditional meaning

The Emperor represents authority, structure, and discipline. He underscores the need for strong foundations in life, whether in career, relationships, or personal development.

He often appears when the seeker is called to step into a leadership role or take decisive action.

The Emperor reflects the archetype of the father figure – one who provides guidance, stability, and protection. He emphasizes the value of rules and structure, and that discipline and consistency are necessary for achieving long-term goals and maintaining order in life.

> "I found Rome a city of bricks and left it a city of marble."
> – Augustus Caesar

Modern interpretation

In the modern world, the Emperor is not a tyrant, but an architect of order who encourages us to take ownership of our lives by establishing clear goals and structures.

A perfect modern archetype is Captain Jean-Luc Picard from *Star Trek: The Next Generation*. His leadership is defined by discipline, strategy, and unwavering accountability for his crew. He fosters stability and navigates chaos by being resolute yet flexible, setting a powerful moral example.

The Emperor challenges us to embody this authority in our own lives: to build a world of purpose, set healthy boundaries, and take command of our destiny with integrity

Reversed

Reversed, the Emperor can signal rigidity, tyranny, or an abuse of power. It might indicate struggles with authority, whether in exerting too much control, or feeling oppressed by external forces. It can also be a warning against stubbornness, and an inability to adapt to change.

A reversed Emperor can also point to a lack of structure or direction, urging the seeker to establish boundaries and restore order. True leadership is not about dominance but about wisdom, fairness, and accountability.

> "A Jedi uses the Force for knowledge and defense, never for attack." – Yoda, <u>The Empire Strikes Back</u>

This is the Emperor's ethical code of conduct, where great power is wielded with discipline for protection and order, never for selfish aggression.

Associations

- *Augustus Caesar*, the first Roman Emperor, ended a century of civil war and established the *Pax Romana* – a long era of stability, order, and prosperity. He embodies the Emperor's role as a master strategist and the architect of a lasting, well-structured society.
- *The cornerstone* is the foundational stone placed at the corner of a building, from which all other stones are set. It symbolizes the Emperor's core function: to provide the essential structure, strength, and alignment upon which a stable and enduring system is built.
- *King Arthur*, the legendary British king, brought order to a chaotic land by creating the fellowship of the Round Table. He was a just leader who established a clear code of conduct and a stable center of power to foster peace and purpose.

> "The best leaders are those most interested in surrounding themselves with assistants and associates smarter than they are." – John C. Maxwell

Leadership is not about standing above others but lifting them up. The Emperor calls for power balanced with wisdom, reminding us that great rulers foster success by empowering those around them.

Final thought

The Emperor reminds us that true power lies in responsibility and the ability to create order amidst chaos.

By embracing structure, discipline, and wise leadership, we build a future of strength, stability, and purpose.

Take command of your life and establish the foundation for lasting success.

5. THE POPE

Guide and teacher of higher knowledge.

Keywords

Spiritual authority, tradition, wisdom, moral leadership.

Practical guidance

- *Seek wisdom* from mentors, teachers, or guides.
- *Honor traditions* that align with your values while remaining open to growth.
- *Reflect on your moral and spiritual beliefs,* ensuring that they shape your actions.
- *Foster unity and understanding* through meaningful dialogue and empathy.
- *Question outdated structures and beliefs* that may hinder your evolution.
- *Lead with integrity*, humility, and a commitment to the greater good.

> "Tradition is not the worship of ashes, but the preservation of fire."
> – Gustav Mahler

Imagery and symbolism

The Pope sits on an elaborate golden throne, wearing richly embroidered robes adorned with sacred symbols. His grand gilded miter signifies his role as the bridge between the divine and mortal realms. In one hand, he holds a tall scepter, symbolizing spiritual authority, while his other hand is raised in a blessing, inviting enlightenment.

Devoted followers kneel in reverence, unified in seeking transmission of sacred teachings. His throne is framed by towering columns within a grand cathedral, befitting structured wisdom and tradition.

At his feet, an open book represents sacred knowledge, while celestial patterns in the stained-glass windows reinforce his connection to higher wisdom. The symmetrical composition highlights the balance of order, discipline, and devotion in seeking enlightenment.

Traditional meaning

The Pope represents spiritual authority, wisdom, and tradition. He signifies the importance of seeking guidance from established institutions, mentors, or sacred texts.

This card often appears when one is called to align with a greater purpose, engage with a community, or deepen their understanding of spiritual truths.

He also embodies moral leadership, urging us to uphold principles that foster harmony and ethical responsibility.

The Pope reminds us that wisdom is gained not only through divine inspiration but also through collective human experience and shared teachings.

Modern interpretation

In the modern world, the Pope represents a trusted guide who bridges tradition and community, combining moral clarity with compassion. He is the mentor who upholds the integrity of an institution.

A secular example is Fred Rogers of *Mister Rogers' Neighborhood*. Through the established structure of his television program, he served as a gentle moral leader for generations. He didn't preach dogma, but used routine and kindness to teach profound lessons of empathy and integrity.

As a humble mentor, he forged a path of personal growth for millions, calling on us to find common ground and lead with our values.

Reversed

Dogmatism, resistance to change, or the questioning of authority. It may point to struggles with conformity or a desire to break free from outdated belief systems.

This card challenges the seeker to evaluate which traditions serve their growth and which may be limiting.

A reversed Pope may also signify hypocrisy or the misuse of power within leadership roles. It serves as a warning to critically assess those in authority and seek guidance that aligns with personal truth and authenticity.

> *"A leader is best when people barely know he exists; when his work is done, they will say: we did it ourselves."* – Lao Tzu

The Pope calls for leadership rooted in wisdom and service.
The best mentors empower others to discover their own truth, guiding without imposing, and leading with humility.

Associations

- *The Mentor archetype* – wisdom, tradition, and guidance, offering knowledge to those who seek it.
- *Chiron* – the wise teacher and healer, guiding others to enlightenment and self-discovery.
- *The Sacred Staff* – a symbol of divine authority, spiritual leadership, and guidance through wisdom.
- *The Pentacle* – sacred knowledge, and the balance of material and divine wisdom, while also embodying the harmony of the Golden Ratio, a mathematical principle found in nature, art, and sacred geometry.

In 325 CE, Emperor Constantine convened the First Council of Nicaea to unify Christian doctrine, shaping the foundation of religious tradition for centuries.

This moment reflects the Pope's role as a guide in establishing wisdom, structure, and shared belief systems. The council balanced preserving tradition with refining teachings, showing that true leadership requires both authority and adaptability.

Final thought

The Pope challenges us to seek higher knowledge and align ourselves with principles that promote wisdom, unity, and spiritual growth. By honoring tradition while remaining open to personal evolution, we integrate the wisdom of the past with the possibilities of the future. Let this card inspire you to be both a student and a teacher.

6. THE LOVERS

The fusion of opposites and the union of energies.

Keywords

Harmony, unity, love, choice, alignment, duality, connection.

Practical guidance

- *Reflect on your values* and ensure your relationships align with them.
- *Embrace open communication* to foster trust and understanding.
- *Recognize the importance of balance* – honor both your needs and those of others.
- *Celebrate relationships* that bring joy and growth.
- *Trust your intuition* when faced with decisions about love and partnership.
- *Invest time and effort in cultivating meaningful connections.*

> **"Life is the sum of all your choices."**
> – Albert Camus

Imagery and symbolism

The Lovers presents a layered narrative of love, choice, and alignment. At the center, a man clad in silver armor stands before two women, each embodying different aspects of life's dualities. The man's posture suggests hesitation, emphasizing the weight of choice and the necessity of balance between instinct and intellect.

Above them, an angel bearing a sword watches over the scene. This celestial presence reminds us that our choices have both earthly and spiritual significance, and consequences.

The figures stand beneath an ancient stone archway, symbolizing transition and the threshold between the interior and external worlds. Beyond them, lush greenery and distant spires evoke the constant presence of the outside world.

> **"Two roads diverged in a wood, and I –
> I took the one less traveled by,
> and that has made all the difference."**
> – Robert Frost, <u>The Road Not Taken</u>

Traditional meaning

The Lovers traditionally signifies harmony, partnership, and the pivotal choices that define our relationships and personal values. The presence of the three figures underscores the theme of decision-making, representing the crossroads where one must choose between different paths or desires. This card reminds us that true unity requires conscious effort, honesty, and alignment with a greater purpose.

At its core, The Lovers addresses the balance of opposites – masculine and feminine, action and intuition, heart and mind. Beyond romance, it highlights the transformative power of love as a force that fosters growth, connection, and unity.

Modern interpretation

In today's world, The Lovers represents a pivotal choice, often one that defines our core values. The card's three figures highlight this complexity.

A powerful modern example is the choice Prince Charles had to make between his public duty with Diana and his private, authentic love for Camilla. This was a classic Lovers crossroads, where any decision would have far-reaching consequences, forcing an alignment between inner truth and outer reality.

This card reminds us that our most powerful choices are those that demand we align our path with our most authentic self, accepting the consequences of that decision.

Reversed

Disharmony, misalignment, or confusion in relationships or choices. It can indicate conflict, indecision, or a struggle to reconcile opposing values. This card warns against superficial connections, and urges deeper introspection.

> **"Trust yourself. You know more than you think you do."**
> *– Benjamin Spock*
>
> Love and connection thrive when we listen to our intuition. The Lovers card urges us to trust our inner voice, recognizing when a relationship or decision aligns with our true path.

One of history's most famous unions, the marriage of Ferdinand of Aragon and Isabella of Castile in 1469, symbolizes The Lovers' theme of unity and choice. Their alliance not only united Spain but also shaped the course of history, demonstrating the power of love and partnership to bring about profound transformation. Like the Lovers, this union reminds us that major choices in relationships and alliances carry both personal and far-reaching consequences.

Associations

- In the myth of *Eros and Psyche,* Psyche's choice to look upon her hidden lover forces her to endure great trials to win him back. A true union requires moving beyond initial harmony, through conscious choice.
- *The Judgment of Paris* – in the Greek myth, a prince's choice between three goddesses leads directly to the Trojan War, embodying the Lovers' theme of a pivotal decision with far-reaching consequences.
- *The crossroads* – always a point of fateful decision and transition, representing the card's central theme of choosing between different paths or desires.

The Lovers card often appears during a moment of significant choice, reflecting *the psychological theory of cognitive dissonance.* This theory describes the mental discomfort we feel when holding conflicting beliefs or when our actions don't align with our values. The card frequently represents a crossroads where any decision—whether between partners, career paths, or personal philosophies—will create this internal tension.

Final thought

The Lovers is a reminder that love, unity, and choice shape our lives. By embracing authenticity and aligning our decisions with our higher selves, we can forge deep, meaningful connections that elevate us. Let this card inspire you to honor both the joys and challenges of love. Trust in its transformative power to guide you toward fulfillment and harmony.

7. THE CHARIOT

Triumph through mastery and focused intent.

Keywords

Willpower, determination, victory, control, ambition, movement, focus, mastery, progress.

Practical guidance

- *Maintain focus.* Define your goals and keep them in sight, avoiding distractions that may hinder progress.
- *Assert control.* Take charge of your circumstances by making deliberate and informed decisions.
- *Balance opposing forces.* Recognize and harmonize conflicting aspects of your life or personality to create a unified path forward.
- *Embrace determination.* Face challenges with unwavering commitment, perseverance, and courage.
- *Reflect on motivation.* Evaluate your intentions to ensure that they align with your desires and values.

Imagery and symbolism

The Chariot showcases a determined charioteer standing within an ornately crafted chariot, drawn by two contrasting horses – one dark, one light – symbolizing opposing forces that must be controlled. Clad in gleaming armor, he firmly grips the reins, representing mastery over these forces and disciplined focus.

The chariot itself is adorned with celestial symbols, reinforcing divine guidance and a journey aligned with higher purpose. Its spinning wheels emphasize rapid movement and unstoppable momentum.

Above the chariot, a starry canopy represents cosmic influence and higher wisdom. The overall composition reflects the balance between control and adaptability, reminding us that true mastery lies in harmonizing competing energies toward a unified goal.

Traditional meaning

Victory, self-mastery, and determination. The Chariot signifies overcoming obstacles through sheer willpower, and resolute, disciplined focus.

This card often appears when one is required to take control of a situation, assert authority, and move forward with confidence. The Chariot calls for strategic thinking, unwavering commitment, and the ability to navigate challenges with strength and clarity.

> **Alexander the Great's unyielding ambition**
> Alexander the Great's conquests demonstrate the Chariot's pursuit of victory and dominance. With a clear vision and extraordinary leadership, he expanded his empire beyond expectations, showing that mastery over oneself and one's circumstances leads to monumental success.

Modern interpretation

In today's world, the Chariot symbolizes the focused drive required to achieve victory in a complex environment by harnessing opposing forces through sheer willpower.

A modern political campaign is a perfect Chariot journey. The candidate, as the charioteer, must control conflicting factions and a chaotic news cycle – the two horses pulling them forward. Success demands firm focus, a clear message, and the relentless determination to overcome obstacles.

This card encourages us to take the reins of our own ambitions with the same strategic clarity, driving forward with the confidence and resolve necessary to achieve our goals.

Reversed

A lack of direction, internal conflict, or a loss of control.

This reversal might indicate hesitation, impulsivity, or difficulty in harnessing personal power. This card warns against reckless ambition, reminding us that discipline and planning are necessary for sustainable success.

A reversed Chariot can also signal resistance to change, self-doubt, or an inability to control competing priorities.

Associations

- *The Roman Triumph* – a parade celebrating victory, recognition, and the disciplined pursuit of excellence.
- *Ben-Hur's chariot race.* In the iconic scene from literature and film, the protagonist, driven by an iron will, must control his powerful horses to achieve a life-or-death victory. It is a literal and dramatic embodiment of the Chariot's triumph through mastery and focused intent.
- *The Space Race* – the Cold War competition between the US and USSR to achieve spaceflight superiority. It reflects the Chariot's immense ambition and determination, harnessing complex, opposing forces – political, scientific, industrial – and directing them with a singular focus toward a monumental goal.
- *Phaethon and the Sun Chariot* – in the Greek myth, Phaethon attempts to drive his father's sun chariot. However, he lacks the control and mastery to handle the powerful horses and nearly destroys the world, serving as a cautionary tale of the reversed Chariot's unchecked ambition.

Harriet Tubman's unstoppable drive

Harriet Tubman embodied the Chariot's perseverance, leading enslaved people to freedom through the Underground Railroad.

Her courage, strategic planning, and resilience turned adversity into triumph, proving that focused willpower can overcome even the most formidable barriers.

Final thought

The Chariot is a reminder of the incredible strength that emerges when we align our willpower with purposeful action and clarity of intent.

It calls upon us to seize the reins of our lives, assert control, and navigate with unwavering confidence, even in the face of daunting challenges. Here is a powerful invitation to pursue goals with steadfast determination.

8. JUSTICE

The embodiment of equilibrium, ethical alignment, and karmic balance.

Keywords

Balance, fairness, truth, accountability, impartiality, law, karma, equality, moral clarity, ethical wisdom.

Practical guidance

- *Seek clarity.* Gather all the facts and consider multiple perspectives before making a decision.
- *Act with integrity.* Align your actions with your values, even when it is inconvenient.
- *Strive for balance.* Weigh all sides of an issue thoughtfully to reach a just resolution.
- *Promote fairness.* Advocate for justice in personal, professional, and community life.
- *Remember karma.* Understand that actions, positive or negative, create lasting effects.

> **"The arc of the moral universe is long, but it bends toward justice."**
> *– Martin Luther King Jr.*

Imagery and symbolism

Justice sits on an ornate throne, embodying wisdom and impartiality. Her steady gaze reflects her commitment to truth and fairness.

In her right hand, she holds an inverted sword, symbolizing introspection, restraint, and the need for careful deliberation before taking action. In her left, balanced scales emphasize her role as an arbiter of truth. Behind her, an arched structure evokes divine order, while a golden halo reinforces enlightenment.

The solemn setting creates an atmosphere of contemplation. Every element highlights the balance between action and reflection, strength and compassion, reminding us that true justice integrates wisdom with empathy.

Traditional meaning

Truth, fairness, and the importance of ethical decision-making. Accountability, urging individuals to take responsibility for their actions and accept their consequences.

Historically, Justice is associated with law, governance, and moral philosophy. It highlights the necessity of objective judgment, self-awareness, and the wisdom to navigate complex moral dilemmas.

> "The law is reason, free from passion."
> – Aristotle (quoted in *Legally Blonde*)
>
> True justice should be based on rational thought, not personal emotions, ensuring fairness and integrity.

Modern interpretation

In our modern world, Justice often represents the slow and difficult process of reckoning with historical atrocities. It is the unwavering commitment to truth and accountability, even decades after the fact.

The Khmer Rouge Tribunal in Cambodia is a powerful modern example. This international court was established to prosecute the senior leaders responsible for the Cambodian genocide of the 1970s. The lengthy trials were not about vengeance, but about creating a meticulous legal record and holding power to account.

This embodies the card's solemn promise that the scales of justice eventually balance, however long and painful the wait.

Reversed

Imbalance, dishonesty, or evasion of responsibility. It may suggest bias, corruption, or manipulation, either in personal choices or within larger institutions. This card warns against unfair treatment and the refusal to confront difficult truths.

A reversed Justice can point to internal struggles – conflict between one's values and actions. It calls for introspection, urging honesty in facing uncomfortable realities.

Additionally, it may signal systemic injustices requiring action and advocacy.

> **"If you want justice, you've come to the wrong place."**
> – Tyrion Lannister, <u>Game of Thrones</u>
>
> A harsh but honest reflection on the imperfections of human justice and the realities of power.

Associations

- In the biblical story, *King Solomon* discerns the true mother of a child by ordering it to be cut in two. This tale is the archetypal example of using wisdom and psychological insight to cut through deception and arrive at a fair and truthful outcome.

- *Newton's Third Law of Motion* is the scientific principle that for every action, there is an equal and opposite reaction. This is an ideal metaphor for the card's theme that all deeds have consequences, and that the universe naturally seeks equilibrium.

- In the Greek play *Antigone*, the protagonist defies the law of the state to follow a higher moral duty. Her story explores the profound conflict between human rules and divine justice, embodying the card's call to align with one's principles, even when faced with consequences.

> **The Code of Hammurabi – The first written law**
>
> One of the earliest known legal codes, Hammurabi's laws established principles of justice and accountability. Like the Justice card, the Code emphasized fairness, consequences for actions, and the idea that laws should guide a balanced society.

Final thought

Justice is both a mirror and a compass, urging us to seek truth, act with integrity, and uphold fairness.

She reminds us that ethical choices shape both personal and collective harmony. Whether facing personal dilemmas or broader societal issues, this card calls for wisdom, courage, and moral clarity in all actions.

JUSTICE / 43

9. THE HERMIT

The seeker of inner truth and wisdom, embracing the path of enlightenment.

Keywords

Introspection, solitude, wisdom, inner guidance, enlightenment, reflection, spiritual journey, self-discovery, quiet contemplation.

Practical guidance

- *Prioritize reflection.* Dedicate time to solitude and introspection to gain clarity about your goals and values.
- *Seek guidance.* Connect with a mentor or trusted individual who can provide insight and perspective.
- *Embrace stillness.* Create space for quiet contemplation, letting go of distractions to focus on your inner journey.
- *Balance solitude and connection.* Know when to step out and engage with others, sharing your insights.
- *Trust your inner light.* Rely on your intuition and inner wisdom to navigate life's uncertainties.
- *Set boundaries.* Protect your energy by limiting distractions and external demands.
- *Document your growth.* Keep a journal to track your thoughts, feelings, and progress.

> "The mind is not a vessel to be filled, but a fire to be kindled." – Plutarch
>
> Like The Hermit's lantern, knowledge is a light that must be nurtured, illuminating the way forward.

> "Knowledge can be communicated, but not wisdom. One can find it, live it, be fortified by it, do wonders through it, but one cannot communicate and teach it."
> – Hermann Hesse, <u>Siddhartha</u>
>
> This captures the Hermit's core truth: that genuine wisdom is not received from others, but is discovered through a personal, internal journey of experience and reflection.

Imagery and symbolism

The Hermit stands on a jagged, snow-covered peak, symbolizing his journey toward enlightenment. His dark, weathered robes embody wisdom and solitude, while his steady gaze reflects deep introspection. In his outstretched hand, a golden lantern glows, cutting through the darkness – representing the wisdom gained through self-reflection. His lowered hood emphasizes his inward journey, while golden strands of energy and power emanate from him.

Glowing lanterns cover the mountainside, representing seekers following their own paths. In the distance, a golden-lit city symbolizes the material world, contrasting with the Hermit's retreat into higher knowledge.

Traditional meaning

A period of introspection and self-discovery. It urges retreat from external distractions to focus on internal wisdom.

As the sage or mentor archetype, the Hermit reminds us that true growth often requires contemplation and patience.

This card also encourages acceptance of the journey's natural rhythm, understanding that insight unfolds in its own time. Trust in the process of personal enlightenment

> Characters such as Prospero from *The Tempest* and Obi-Wan Kenobi in *Star Wars* reflect the Hermit's wisdom. Both retreat into solitude to gain insight, later emerging to guide others. Their journeys echo the card's theme – true wisdom is often forged in seclusion.

Modern interpretation

In today's fast-paced world, The Hermit calls for moments of pause and reflection. Stepping away from distractions fosters clarity and personal growth. Solitude is not just isolation, but an opportunity to reconnect with one's true self.

The Hermit also represents mentorship and the wisdom shared across generations. Whether seeking guidance or becoming a beacon for others, this card highlights the reciprocal nature of knowledge – what we learn in solitude can illuminate the paths of those who follow.

Reversed

Reversed, the Hermit warns against excessive withdrawal or isolation, for that can lead to loneliness and stagnation. It can indicate avoidance of responsibilities or fears, keeping the seeker from necessary growth.

> **"Whosoever is delighted in solitude is either a wild beast or a god."**
> – *Aristotle*
>
> Solitude is not for everyone, but for those who seek wisdom, it is a sacred path to enlightenment.

It can also signal resistance to introspection, where truths are ignored rather than faced. Alternatively, it may mark the end of a period of solitude, urging re-engagement with the world and the sharing of hard-earned wisdom. The lesson is *balance* – between inner reflection and external connection.

Associations

- *Siddhartha's quest for enlightenment.* Before becoming the Buddha, Prince Siddhartha left his worldly life to embark on a solitary spiritual journey; a perfect embodiment of the Hermit's path to enlightenment.
- *The lighthouse keeper* lives in solitude, maintaining a powerful light to guide others through darkness. This mirrors the Hermit, who retreats to find his own inner wisdom, which then serves as a beacon for other seekers.
- *Yoda's exile on Dagobah.* The Jedi Master from *Star Wars* withdraws from a galaxy in turmoil to live a life of quiet contemplation, later emerging as a wise mentor to guide a new generation on its spiritual journey.

Final thought

The Hermit teaches that the greatest journeys are those taken within. By embracing solitude, reflecting on life's deeper questions, and trusting in our inner world, we uncover truths that lead to personal growth.

Regardless of where we are, the Hermit's lantern inspires trust in our path, and faith in the answers that await us.

10. THE WHEEL

Cycles of fate, change, and destiny in motion.

Keywords

Fate, cycles, luck, destiny, turning points, karma, unpredictability, change, opportunity, adaptation.

Practical guidance

- *Embrace change.* Life moves in cycles. Navigate the highs and lows with grace.
- *Recognize patterns.* Identify recurring themes in your life and their influence.
- *Stay adaptable.* Resilience helps you flow with shifting circumstances.
- *Trust the process.* Even in uncertainty, trust that events unfold as they should.
- *Take the initiative.* While fate plays a role, choices influence the wheel's turn.
- *Learn from history.* The past offers insight into present and future cycles.
- *Prepare for the unexpected.* Fortune shifts in an instant – stay ready for new opportunities.

Imagery and symbolism

The Wheel dominates the composition, an intricate celestial mechanism adorned with ancient symbols, zodiac signs, and cosmic engravings. At its center, a golden pentacle symbolizes balance amid change, the unchanging core of existence. The wheel's many spokes suggest infinite possibilities and paths.

> **"When the winds of change blow, some build walls, others build windmills."**
> – Chinese proverb
>
> How you respond to change determines whether you thrive or struggle. Adaptability is key.

Atop the wheel, a regal figure with curved horns presides over fate. Figures ascend and descend the wheel's sides, embodying fortune's rise and fall. Below, mythic beasts – a dragon and a celestial horse – intertwine in motion, representing chaos and order.

Cosmic clouds swirl in the background, evoking the vast, unpredictable nature of fate. Stars and planetary symbols reflect unseen forces shaping events. The golden glow suggests that even in uncertainty, wisdom is found by aligning with life's greater rhythm.

Traditional meaning

Historically, the Wheel symbolizes fate's unpredictability. In medieval and Renaissance art, Fortuna's wheel turned without bias – elevating rulers one moment, casting them down the next. This card teaches that all things are temporary, and both triumph and hardship are part of life's design.

> "All the world's a stage, and all the men and women merely players."
> – *William Shakespeare*
>
> Life's cycles make us actors in fate's grand design. Understanding this helps us play our roles wisely. While we may not control the script, we can choose how we perform our part.

Modern interpretation

In today's world, the Wheel represents life's unpredictable cycles, reminding us that nothing is static. The 2008 global financial crisis was a powerful turn of the Wheel. This sudden collapse shifted fortunes on a massive scale, showing that even stable systems are subject to unpredictable change.

The Wheel highlights such turning points, and urges adaptability in the face of unexpected twists. Those who embrace transformation will thrive, while those who resist the wheel's turn will struggle.

Reversed

Resistance to change, misfortune, or feeling trapped in cycles. It suggests a lack of control, where external events feel overwhelming.

This card in reverse may indicate a need to break negative patterns or rethink choices. It calls for inner work to change one's relationship with fate – stepping out of passivity into active engagement with life.

The Psychology of Control and Luck

Studies in psychology show that people with an *internal* locus of control – who believe their actions shape their fate – tend to be more successful and resilient. Meanwhile, those with an *external* locus of control – who see life as dictated by outside forces – often feel helpless when faced with challenges. The Wheel reminds us that while fate plays a role, we have the power to influence how we respond to life's twists and turns.

A well-known example is Thomas Edison, whose persistence led to the invention of the light bulb. Despite thousands of failed attempts, he reframed each failure as a step toward success.

His ability to see setbacks as part of the learning process exemplifies how mindset and adaptability influence fortune – that those who believe that their actions shape their fate tend to be more successful and resilient.

Associations

- *The Fate Weaver* archetype – symbolizing cycles, destiny, and fortune.
- *The Moirai* – the Greek Fates who spin, measure, and cut life's thread.
- *The number 10* – completion, transition, and new cycles.
- *The Ouroboros*, the snake eating its own tail – eternal cycles of renewal and change.

"Can't repeat the past? Why of course you can!"
– The Great Gatsby

Fortune is unpredictable. What matters is how you ride the ups and downs. Jay Gatsby in *The Great Gatsby* believed he could bend fate to his will, only to find himself undone by forces beyond his control.

His story serves as a reminder that while ambition can drive success, external circumstances often shape our destinies in ways we cannot foresee.

Final thought

The Wheel reminds us that life's only certainty is change. Whether rising or falling, each turn of the wheel brings new opportunities and challenges. Embrace the cycles, act with awareness, and trust that even the unexpected serves a greater purpose. Every twist of fate is a chance for growth and transformation, leading us toward new beginnings.

11. STRENGTH

The embodiment of power in gentleness and harmony, symbolizing mastery of the self.

Keywords

Inner strength, compassion, courage, patience, resilience, balance, self-control, grace under pressure.

Practical guidance

- *Cultivate patience.* Approach challenges with calm determination, avoiding rash or impulsive decisions.
- *Trust in your strength.* Believe in your ability to overcome obstacles, no matter how insurmountable they may seem.
- *Balance power and compassion.* Lead with empathy, knowing true strength comes from understanding.
- *Embrace vulnerability.* Openness and honesty are signs of courage, not weakness.
- *Practice self-control.* Manage emotions and impulses, maintaining clarity in difficult situations.
- *Stay grounded.* Connect with your inner resources through meditation or time in nature.
- *Empower others.* Use your strength to uplift and inspire those around you.
- *Celebrate small victories.* Recognize the courage it takes to face even minor challenges.
- *Confront fears.* Growth comes from stepping beyond your comfort zone.
- *Create harmony.* Seek balance in your relationships, fostering mutual respect.

> **The quiet power of Rosa Parks**
>
> Rosa Parks' refusal to give up her seat was an act of immense strength – not through aggression, but through quiet defiance and resilience. Strength teaches that courage often speaks in whispers rather than shouts.

Imagery and symbolism

The Strength card shows a moment of profound harmony between human and beast. A serene woman, adorned in golden jewelry, radiates calm confidence as she gently embraces a majestic lion.

The lion, powerful yet at peace, rests its head in trust. It symbolizes primal instincts, emotions, and raw strength, tamed not by force but with patience and understanding. This union represents the triumph of inner mastery over brute force.

Traditional meaning

Traditionally, Strength reveals the power of inner mastery, a concept mirrored in Carl Jung's psychology. The woman calmly engaging the lion is a powerful symbol of integrating the 'shadow self' – our primal instincts, passions, and fears. The goal is not to conquer this inner beast with brute force, but to meet it with compassion and understanding, transforming its raw energy into a source of conscious power.

This card calls for this exact kind of courage and emotional wisdom. It teaches that true resilience is forged through patience and self-control, allowing you to navigate challenges with a quiet, unshakeable grace. True strength is the ability to face your own inner lion and befriend it, channeling its power with a gentle and knowing hand.

Modern interpretation

In a world that often equates strength with dominance, this card highlights the power of compassion and resilience.

A powerful modern example is Dr. Martin Luther King Jr.'s philosophy of nonviolent resistance. The civil rights movement demonstrated immense courage by meeting aggression not with force, but with patience and unwavering self-control. This approach showed that true strength is found in deep conviction and the grace to meet hatred with a higher ideal – and that our greatest power lies in our inner resolve.

> **"Courage is the most important of all the virtues because without courage, you can't practice any other virtue consistently."** – *Maya Angelou*
>
> True strength comes from the courage required to act with patience, resilience, and compassion.

Reversed

Self-doubt, impatience, or emotional overwhelm. Impulsive actions or inner turmoil, urging a return to calm and self-trust.

Strength reversed can also signal using force rather than understanding, calling for a reassessment of one's approach.

This position may also indicate an unwillingness to confront personal fears. It encourages growth through introspection, urging the seeker to embrace self-awareness and patience.

Associations

- *Daniel in the Lions' Den.* A prophet's calm faith and inner resolve pacify a den of lions. This mirrors the card's imagery and its core theme of courage and self-control triumphing over primal force.
- *Mahatma Gandhi and Satyagraha* Gandhi's philosophy of *nonviolent resistance* is a real-world embodiment of the Strength card. It is a strategy built on immense patience, moral courage, and self-control, proving that the greatest power can be found in gentleness, not aggression.

> **"The best fighter is never angry."** – *Lao Tzu, Tao Te Ching*
>
> This ancient wisdom reflects this card's lesson – the greatest power is found in calm self-control and emotional mastery, not in aggression.

Final thought

Strength reminds us that power is not about force but about self-awareness, patience, and the ability to act with compassion.

True strength is the quiet confidence that transforms fear into trust and struggle into wisdom. Strength is not measured by what we can control, but by how we choose to respond to life's challenges.

12. THE HANGED MAN

A moment of stillness before transformation, offering a new perspective between the known and the unknown.

Keywords

Surrender, perspective, sacrifice, letting go, suspension, patience, transformation.

Practical guidance

- *Actions have consequences.* Remember karma.
- *Embrace stillness.* Allow yourself time to pause and reflect, even if it feels uncomfortable.
- *Shift perspective.* Challenge assumptions and look at challenges from a different angle.
- *Let go of control.* Trust the unfolding of events rather than forcing outcomes.
- *Sacrifice for growth.* Identify and release beliefs or habits that no longer serve you.
- *Reframe challenges.* View obstacles as opportunities for insight and resilience.

> **"You have power over your mind – not outside events. Realize this, and you will find strength."**
> – Marcus Aurelius
> The Stoic approach to surrender.

Imagery and symbolism

A young man hangs upside down from a wooden beam suspended between two trees. His expression shows acceptance and resignation rather than distress, highlighting the theme of voluntary surrender.

The misty forest around him suggests introspection and uncertainty, while the bare trees reflect the necessity of releasing the old before growth can occur.

Historically, in northern Italy, those hung upside down were being punished for treason – this card was sometimes called the Traitor – yet this Hanged Man reclaims this image with a message of transformation through surrender, reminding us that letting go leads to greater wisdom.

The psychology of letting go

Psychologists emphasize the power of cognitive reframing – the ability to change one's perspective of a situation. The Hanged Man embodies this shift, teaching that seeing life from a new angle can unlock deeper understanding and peace.

Letting go is not just an act of surrender but an active step toward growth. When we release control over external circumstances, we gain mastery over our inner world.

Studies in acceptance and commitment therapy (ACT) suggest that resisting change often leads to suffering, while embracing uncertainty fosters resilience. When we detach from rigid thinking, we allow insight to emerge naturally, rather than forcing solutions.

History also provides a lesson in this philosophy. The ancient Taoist principle of *Wu Wei*, or effortless action, teaches that the most effective way to navigate life is by aligning with its natural flow. The Hanged Man reflects this wisdom, demonstrating that patience and adaptability open doors that force never could.

Traditional meaning

Early Italian tarot decks depicted the Hanged Man suspended by one foot, referencing the medieval punishment for traitors. Over time, this symbol of public disgrace transformed into one of profound wisdom and spiritual enlightenment. Taking on the idea of willing sacrifice, it came to mirror themes in Christian mysticism and Renaissance thought, where moments of contemplation and suffering are seen as gateways to divine insight.

Modern interpretation

In today's fast-paced world, the Hanged Man's power of pause is an antidote to constant hustle. This is seen in the modern ritual of a career sabbatical or a gap year – a voluntary suspension of the expected path. While it may look like stalled progress to outsiders, this period of surrender is a necessary phase of growth. The Hanged Man teaches that true freedom comes from letting go of control, reassessing priorities, and trusting that a transformative new perspective will emerge from the stillness.

> "The real voyage of discovery consists not in seeking new landscapes, but in having new eyes." – *Marcel Proust*

Reversed

Reversed, the Hanged Man suggests resistance to change or a reluctance to let go. It warns against clinging to old patterns that no longer serve us. This position may also indicate stagnation – being stuck in indecision or avoidance.

Alternatively, it can signal that the period of suspension is coming to an end, urging action based on the insights gained during reflection.

Associations

- *The liminal space:* an airport transit lounge is the threshold between your origin and your destination. Time seems to stretch and distort. With all forward action paused, you are forced into a state of pure transition – a waiting period for introspection and observation before the next phase of your journey begins.

- *Odin*, the Nordic god, hung from the world tree Yggdrasil for nine days and nights, to gain divine knowledge. His sacrifice led to wisdom – showing that surrender can lead to transformation.

> "When I let go of what I am, I become what I might be."
> – *Lao Tzu*
>
> This Taoist wisdom perfectly captures the card's core lesson that true growth requires the voluntary sacrifice and surrender of our current identity. Let go.

Final thought

The Hanged Man teaches us that surrender is not weakness, but wisdom. By embracing stillness, letting go of control, and shifting our perspective, we open ourselves to transformation. This card reminds us that discomfort and uncertainty are often the gateways to deeper understanding and personal growth.

13. DEATH

*A profound transition, marking the end
of one cycle and the beginning of another.*

Keywords

Transformation, endings, renewal, release, inevitability, surrender, cycles, transition, rebirth, closure.

Practical guidance

- *Embrace change.* Let go of what no longer serves you. Make room for new growth.
- *Release the past.* Holding onto outdated patterns prevents transformation – trust the process of renewal.
- *Face endings with grace.* Change is inevitable; meeting it with acceptance leads to growth.
- *See opportunity in loss.* What seems like an ending often leads to a better beginning.
- *Let go of fear.* Transformation is a natural and necessary part of life.
- *Trust in rebirth.* Every ending is a doorway to something new.

> "It is not death that a man should fear, but never beginning to live."
> – Marcus Aurelius
>
> Even in endings, the philosophy of Stoicism reminds us that life is about transformation, not loss.

Imagery and symbolism

Untitled, unnumbered, Death, a skeletal figure cloaked in black, wields a massive scythe. This is not a harbinger of doom, but an agent of transformation. The skeletal form represents what is left after all superficial layers have been stripped away – the essential self, free from illusion.

The scythe is the tool of harvest, severing the old to make way for the new. Around Death's feet lie remnants of the past: lifeless disfigured heads and limbs, symbolizing the inevitable conclusion of all things. Yet, beneath the decay the grass still grows, a sign of rebirth and the promise of renewal.

Traditional meaning

In early tarot, such as the Visconti-Sforza deck, the card depicted simply a skeleton wielding a scythe.

In medieval Europe, the *Danse Macabre* (Dance of Death) was a common motif, portraying Death as the great equalizer, sparing no one regardless of status. Change is inevitable for all – and resistance only prolongs suffering.

Kali's mythology teaches that destruction is not an end, but a transformative process. In one tale, she emerges during a great battle against demons, unleashing chaos and slaying her enemies with relentless energy.

Yet, when the battle is won, she is calmed by Shiva, reminding us that even the most intense destruction must eventually give way to peace and regeneration.

Modern interpretation

In a society that often resists change, Death serves here as a reminder that endings are not to be feared. Whether it's the conclusion of a relationship, a career shift, or a personal transformation, Death demands acceptance and adaptation.

This card is also a call to release fear. The unknown can be unsettling, but Death reassures us that every ending leads to a fresh start. By letting go of what no longer serves us, we allow for renewal and transformation.

Reversed

Resistance to change, or an unwillingness to let go of the past. It may indicate stagnation, fear of transformation, or avoidance of necessary endings.

This reversal commands self-reflection: what are you clinging to that no longer serves you?

> "What we call the beginning is often the end. And to make an end is to make a beginning. The end is where we start from."
> – T.S. Eliot, <u>Little Gidding</u>

Associations

- *The Phoenix* is an ancient symbol of transformation, cyclically burning itself to ashes, only to rise again. Like the Death card, it teaches that from destruction comes renewal, and every ending carries the promise of rebirth.

- *The psychological process of letting go.* Psychologists emphasize that grieving an ending is essential for growth. Whether mourning a relationship, a job, or an identity, the process of acceptance, adaptation, and renewal mirrors the lessons of Death. Letting go is not just about loss – it is about making space for something new.

- *Hades, ruler of the underworld,* is not a figure of evil, but the Greek god who rules the underworld as a solemn custodian of transition. He represents the impersonal and inevitable force of the Death card, which guides all things through profound change as part of a natural cycle, not as an act of malice.

> "The snake which cannot cast its skin has to die. As well the minds which are prevented from changing their opinions; they cease to be mind." – *Friedrich Nietzsche*

> The Black Death devastated Europe in the 14th century, yet in its wake came profound societal change. Feudalism weakened, wages and living standards rose, and the Renaissance emerged. Like Death, destruction cleared the way for rebirth and progress.

Final thought

The Death card is not a warning but an invitation to surrender to change, embrace endings, and trust in the process of transformation. It teaches that every loss makes space for new beginnings, and that in letting go, we allow ourselves to grow.

The Norse god Baldur, whose death marked the end of an age and the promise of a reborn world, reflects this lesson.

14. TEMPERANCE

*A symbol of balance, integration,
and the harmony of opposing forces.*

Keywords
Balance, harmony, moderation, patience, blending, healing, purpose, divine guidance, renewal, integration.

Practical guidance

- *Strive for balance.* Identify areas of excess and take conscious steps to restore harmony.
- *Practice moderation.* Avoid extremes; measured action leads to sustainable growth.
- *Blend opposites.* Integrate reason and emotion, action and rest, discipline and flexibility.
- *Trust the process.* Progress takes time; embrace patience as part of the journey.

> "The meeting of two personalities is like the contact of two chemical substances: if there is any reaction, both are transformed."
> – Carl Jung

Imagery & symbolism

An angelic figure with large outstretched wings exudes serenity and grace. Her bare feet touch both both a flowing stream, symbolizing emotional depth and intuition, and the solid earth, representing stability. The golden glow around her head radiates divine wisdom, showing her source in the higher realms.

She holds two ornate golden vessels, pouring water from one to the other in a continuous, unbroken stream. She is performing alchemy – the blending of opposites into a harmonious whole. The symbolism reflects the delicate art of measured balance, where action and stillness, intuition and logic, spiritual and material, are all woven together seamlessly.

Behind her, the landscape is lush and thriving, with a waterfall feeding the stream at her feet. Temperance reassures us that balance is ultimately inevitable.

Traditional meaning

Temperance signifies moderation and balance in all aspects of life. It speaks of healing, renewal, and self-discipline, urging patience and care when navigating challenges.

Historically, this card has been associated with the philosophy of alchemy, symbolizing the process of refining and transforming experiences into wisdom.

In the earliest medieval tarots, Temperance was depicted as a woman mixing two substances, representing the delicate art of blending opposites to achieve stability. The card teaches that life's greatest lessons come not from extremes but from the steady integration of seemingly conflicting elements.

Psychological balance: Jung & individuation

Jung's process of individuation is about integrating all aspects of the psyche – the conscious and unconscious, rational and emotional. Individuation is the path toward self-realization, where a person unites their inner opposites – logic and intuition, strength and vulnerability, the known and the mysterious. Jung believed that only by embracing our hidden, suppressed, or ignored aspects can we achieve wholeness.

In Jungian analysis, the shadow self – our repressed, less favorable traits – must be recognized and integrated rather than denied.

Temperance mirrors this journey, reminding us that true harmony comes from acknowledging and blending all facets of the self. The angel carefully mixes two elements, just as a balanced psyche integrates its disparate forces to create a stable and coherent being. Just as the angel pours liquid between two vessels, true personal growth flows through the unification of all aspects of self.

Modern interpretation

In a world of extremes, Temperance is the art of healing integration, embodied by the Japanese practice of *Kintsugi*.

By mending broken pottery with gold, it creates a more beautiful whole from imperfection. Temperance urges us to patiently blend our own opposing parts – work and rest, logic and intuition – to find a balanced, resilient purpose.

Reversed

When reversed, Temperance warns of imbalance, excess, or impulsive behavior. It may signal overindulgence, a lack of self-control, or resistance to necessary moderation.

This card urges a reassessment of priorities, encouraging a return to measured, mindful choices. It may also indicate stagnation, reminding the seeker that balance is not passive – it requires ongoing effort and adjustment.

Associations

- *Iris* – the Greek messenger goddess bridges heaven and earth, representing the perfect harmony, balance, and unity achieved by Temperance.
- *The Taoist principle of balancing yin and yang*. It reflects Temperance's harmony achieved by integrating the dual forces of nature.
- *The art of Alchemy* – the symbolic transformation of the self through patient integration. The alchemist's work mirrors Temperance by blending opposites for enlightenment.
- *The Golden Mean* was Aristotle's model for a virtuous life, achieved by finding balance between extremes. It champions moderation as the path to fulfillment.

> **"Even the smallest person can change the course of the future."**
> – J.R.R. Tolkien, *The Lord of the Rings*
>
> This reflects the essence of Temperance, reminding us that transformation and balance often begin with the smallest, yet most intentional, steps.

Final thought

Temperance is the art of measured balance – a guiding force that teaches patience, blending, and integration.

It encourages trust in the process of transformation, reminding us that by walking the middle path, we cultivate lasting harmony, balance, and understanding.

15. THE DEVIL

Bondage, temptation – and the challenge of self-mastery.

Keywords

Bondage, temptation, materialism, addiction, illusion, fear, entrapment, shadow self, liberation, transformation.

Practical guidance

- *Identify attachments.* Where are you trapped or controlled?
- *Confront fears.* Face suppressed aspects of yourself with honesty and courage.
- *Recognize illusions.* Question limiting beliefs and narratives.
- *Reclaim power.* Take small, conscious steps toward liberation.
- *Embrace moderation.* Avoid extremes and balance indulgence with mindfulness.
- *Choose freedom.* Understand that self-mastery begins with self-awareness.

> "The chains of habit are too light to be felt until they are too heavy to be broken."
> – Warren Buffett
>
> A reflection on the subtle nature of entrapment; the Devil's theme of unconscious patterns leading to deep-rooted struggles.

Imagery & symbolism

A demonic and monstrous figure towers over two chained acolytes. The creature blends divine and bestial elements; it personifies dominance, cruelty, and appetite.

One hand grips a serpent, a symbol of temptation, hidden wisdom, and transformation, while the other misshapen hand gestures toward the bound figures, suggesting their enslavement and their Master's total control over them.

The two figures in the foreground are only loosely bound by chains; their imprisonment is partly self-imposed. The background enhances this message: a city burns in the distance, signifying the destructive power of unchecked desires. Behind the Devil rises cracked, ancient stonework – these struggles have existed throughout human history.

Traditional meaning

The Devil represents the experience of feeling trapped – whether by external circumstances, toxic relationships, or internal fears and addictions.

It calls attention to the parts of our psyche that thrive in darkness, urging us to confront them rather than avoid them. While it may seem like an ominous sign, this card is an invitation to break free from illusions and reclaim autonomy.

Modern interpretation

In today's world, the Devil warns of the seductive power of illusion and materialism. The infamous Fyre Festival is a perfect modern parable for this card. It used the temptation of an exclusive, luxurious fantasy, promoted through social media, to trap attendees in a reality of chaos and lack. The 'loose chains' binding the festival-goers were their own desires to buy into a flawless, curated image.

The festival's public collapse was a collective moment of shadow work, exposing the emptiness behind the glamour. This card challenges us to have a similar moment of honest awareness: to see our own attachments to illusions, confront the destructive habits they create, and recognize that we hold the power to simply walk away.

> *"One does not become enlightened by imagining figures of light, but by making the darkness conscious."* – Carl Jung
>
> True liberation comes not from ignoring our shadow self, but from confronting it with courage and awareness.

Reversed

A breaking of chains and a step toward liberation. The seeker is in the process of overcoming addictions, breaking free from limiting beliefs, or stepping away from toxic influences.

This reversal is a card of hope and personal empowerment, reminding us that transformation is possible.

However, the reversal can also indicate denial or repression – a refusal to face the truth or confront one's shadow self. In such cases, it serves as a warning that true freedom comes only through self-awareness and courage.

The Devil is more than just an internal struggle; it is also a reflection of the forces – both within and without – that seek to control, deceive, or manipulate. This card demands that we look beyond illusions, and ask where the chains truly lie – are they within our own minds, or is it external forces that keep us bound? By confronting these hidden aspects, we take the first step toward true autonomy.

A well-known example of this theme can be found in the film *The Matrix*. Neo, the main character, initially lives under the illusion that his world is real, unaware that he is trapped inside a system designed to control him.

The Devil embodies the same deception – an unseen force convincing us that we are powerless when, in truth, we hold the ability to break free. Just as Neo awakens to the reality of his captivity and struggles to escape, this card demands that we recognize the chains that bind us, and reclaim ourselves.

Associations

- *Faust's pact with Mephistopheles* – the archetypal story of trading one's soul for worldly pleasure, embodying the bondage that results from unchecked desire.
- *Plato's allegory of the cave*: the philosophical allegory of prisoners mistaking shadows for reality, representing self-imposed bondage through illusion. It teaches that liberation begins with awareness.
- *Addiction to social media* is modern slavery; individuals become bound to a cycle of external validation and curated illusions, disconnecting them from their true selves.

Final thought

While the Devil represents the dangers of unchecked desire and self-imposed bondage, it would be naive to assume that evil exists only within the self. History and experience remind us that destructive forces operate beyond personal illusions – manipulative systems, toxic relationships, and predatory influences can all play a role in our captivity.

16. THE TOWER

A turning point forces growth through dramatic transformation – a harbinger of profound insight.

Keywords

Upheaval, sudden change, destruction, revelation, chaos, awakening, liberation, rebuilding, transformation.

Practical guidance

- *Embrace change.* Upheaval is part of life. Adapt and grow.
- *Rebuild wisely.* Construct stronger, more authentic foundations.
- *Find freedom in chaos.* Destruction can break unseen chains.
- *Stay resilient.* Know that turmoil is temporary, and clarity will emerge.

> **"Even the mightiest of towers will one day crumble."**
> – The Lord of the Rings
>
> A fitting reminder that power, empires, and illusions are never permanent. Like the fall of Isengard or Barad-dûr, the Tower represents sudden upheaval which exposes hidden weaknesses and brings necessary transformation.

Imagery and symbolism

The Tower presents a scene of cataclysmic transformation, illustrating the destructive yet purifying power of sudden change. A looming stone tower stands defiantly against a storm-filled sky, only to be struck by lightning, its spires crumbling in fire and debris. This symbolizes the collapse of illusions and the shattering of false foundations.

Two figures fall from the tower, arms flung wide in a mix of terror and surrender. Their descent represents forced release from what once seemed stable, offering both devastation and freedom. The jagged cliffs below reinforce the harsh reality of the painful truths which they are about to face.

In the background, other towers loom, suggesting that no structure – physical, emotional, or ideological – is immune to change.

> "There is a crack, a crack in everything – that's how the light gets in." – Leonard Cohen, Anthem

Traditional meaning

Sudden upheaval, shaking the very core of our beliefs, relationships, or circumstances. What once seemed indestructible is revealed to be fragile, urging us to rebuild on firmer ground. While painful, this process is essential for personal and spiritual evolution.

Historically, the Tower has been linked to hubris and downfall, warning against rigid structures built on falsehoods. It is a reminder of life's impermanence, demanding adaptability, humility, and a willingness to embrace change.

Modern interpretation

In today's world, the Tower represents the sudden shattering of systems we believe are permanent.

The global Covid-19 pandemic, whatever it was, was a profound, collective Tower moment. Overnight, it dismantled seemingly indestructible structures of work, travel, and social life, revealing their true fragility. This upheaval was a painful revelation, challenging us to confront false constructs in our lives – from unsustainable jobs to superficial connections.

While the collapse of the 'old normal' brought chaos, it also cleared the way for radical transformation, forcing us to rebuild our lives in a new reality.

> "You must be ready to burn yourself in your own flame; how could you rise anew if you have not first become ashes?"
> – Friedrich Nietzsche, <u>Thus Spoke Zarathustra</u>

Reversed meaning

Resistance to change, an unwillingness to let go, or denial of an inevitable transformation. Clinging to illusions may prolong suffering rather than prevent it. This card warns that fighting the collapse only deepens the chaos.

Additionally, this reversal can indicate that there is potential to emerge from a crisis, with the worst having passed. Here, the focus shifts to rebuilding – whether in relationships, career, or self-perception.

THE CITY OF DIS
The Tower is reminiscent of the city of Dis from Dante's *Divine Comedy*, which symbolizes the fall of pride, corruption, and false security.

Dante viewed such destruction as an act of divine justice, much like the tarot's lightning-struck tower. Just as his sinners are forced to reckon with their choices, the Tower signifies a dramatic upheaval that strips away falsehoods and forces a confrontation with reality. This destruction is not simple punishment, but a necessary stage on the path to enlightenment, reconstruction, and renewal.

Associations

- *The Tower of Babel* – the biblical allegory of a tower built from human pride that is struck down by divine intervention, representing the destruction that follows arrogant ambition.

- *The fall of the Bastille* – the storming of the French prison that symbolized the sudden, violent, and liberating overthrow of an oppressive and corrupt regime.

- *Hubris in Greek tragedy* was a recurring theme; a hero's excessive pride and defiance of the gods leads to their own sudden and catastrophic downfall.

- *'Creative destruction'* is an economic theory – radical innovation (symbolized by the Tower's lightning strike) destroys old industries and structures to make way for new ones.

Final thoughts

The Tower is not a symbol of despair but of revelation. It reminds us that life's greatest transformations often come from destruction. It challenges us to let go of what no longer serves us, to face the storm with courage, and rebuild with wisdom and authenticity. True enlightenment emerges when we embrace the impermanence of all things and learn to thrive in the face of chaos.

17. THE STAR

A guiding light; serenity and renewal.

Keywords

Hope, renewal, inspiration, serenity, spiritual guidance, clarity, healing, harmony.

Practical guidance

- *Embrace a time of peace and optimism.*
- *Trust in the universe* and allow healing energy to flow.
- *Realign with your true purpose* and let hope guide you forward.
- *Seek moments of solitude* to reconnect with your inner self.
- *Express gratitude for the light* that remains even in dark times.

> "The cosmos is within us. We are made of star-stuff. We are a way for the universe to know itself."
> – Carl Sagan, <u>Cosmos</u>

Imagery and symbolism

A luminous woman kneels by a tranquil stream, pouring water from two vessels. One is golden, its contents flowing onto the dry earth, nourishing the ground with renewal. The other is silver, its water spilling back into the stream, symbolizing the return of wisdom to the eternal cycle.

The woman's expression is serene, her gaze lowered in contemplation, suggesting quiet self-assurance and trust in the unfolding of destiny. Above her, a brilliant star radiates outward, its glow piercing the dark sky – guidance, cosmic wisdom, and divine inspiration. Her bare feet, connected to the ground, reaffirm her role as both celestial and earthly, bridging the divine and the material.

A raven perches on a tree branch, watching silently, a reminder of the balance between light and shadow, the known and the unknown. The presence of the raven, often seen as a messenger between worlds, hints at the dual nature of wisdom – earthly knowledge and spiritual insight.

Traditional meaning

The Star brings calm after the storm, a moment of clarity following upheaval. It represents divine inspiration and inner guidance, reminding us that light always returns even in darkness. In times of despair, the Star offers reassurance that healing is possible and that new opportunities will emerge. It encourages us to trust in the natural cycles of renewal and to embrace the peace that follows turmoil.

> **Astronomer Carl Sagan often spoke of the 'pale blue dot,' referring to Earth's place in the vast cosmos.**
>
> **The Star invites us to take this same perspective – to see beyond momentary struggles, and recognize our connection to something greater.**

Modern interpretation

In an age of uncertainty, the Star is a beacon of resilience, reminding us that clarity often follows chaos.

A perfect modern example is Vincent van Gogh's masterpiece, *The Starry Night*. He painted this iconic image from the window of an asylum, a time of deep personal turmoil and upheaval. From that darkness, he reconnected with a sense of cosmic wonder, creating a universal symbol of hope and inspiration. This card urges us to do the same in our own difficult moments: to trust in our ability to heal, remain open to inspiration, and find our own guiding light.

Reversed

Doubt and disillusionment cloud your vision, making it difficult to see the path ahead. You may feel disconnected from hope or uncertain about your purpose, caught in a cycle of negativity or self-doubt. This card warns against allowing pessimism to take root and urges you to confront what is holding you back. It may also indicate a loss of faith, whether in yourself, others, or the universe. Realign with your inner truth, seek sources of renewal, and trust that clarity will return with time and patience.

Galileo's celestial discoveries challenged existing worldviews and reshaped our understanding of the universe. The Star embodies that same search for truth, pushing us toward enlightenment and broader horizons.

Associations

- *Astraea*, the Greek goddess of the stars, symbolizes purity and renewal.
- *The North Star* – an historical and mythological emblem of direction and purpose.
- *The Age of Exploration* – Celestial navigation led adventurers toward the unknown.
- *Pandora's Box* – in the Greek myth, after all the evils of the world are released from a jar, only one thing remains inside: Hope. This story is a perfect parallel to the Star's appearance after the chaos of the Tower, representing the hope that endures even in the darkest of times.
- *The Renaissance's fascination with the cosmos* – The revival of celestial study and humanist philosophy during the Renaissance mirrors the Star's theme of enlightenment.

> "...and thence we came forth to see again the stars."
> – Dante Alighieri, *Inferno*
>
> This is the final line of the *Inferno*, expressing the profound relief and renewal of emerging from the deepest darkness back into the light of hope and guidance.

Final thoughts

Hope is not passive; it is an active force that lights the way forward, reminding us that every challenge holds the potential for renewal.

The Star reminds us that even in darkness, hope endures. It calls us to trust the process of healing, embrace new possibilities, and allow inspiration to guide us.

18. THE MOON

Where illusion and intuition meet in the shadows.

Keywords

Illusion, intuition, uncertainty, dreams, subconscious, mystery, deception, imagination, transformation.

Practical guidance

- *Trust your intuition*, even when logic fails.
- *Be wary of deception.* Things may not be as they appear.
- *Pay attention to dreams and symbols*; your subconscious is speaking.
- *Move forward despite uncertainty*, knowing clarity will come in time.
- *Embrace mystery and transformation* rather than fearing them.

> "We are all like the bright moon, we still have our darker side." – *Kahlil Gibran*

> "The moon is a loyal companion. It never leaves. It's always there, watching, steadfast, knowing us in our light and dark moments."
> – *Tahereh Mafi*
>
> This captures the Moon's role as a guide through uncertainty, even when we cannot see the way forward.

Imagery and symbolism

A surreal landscape is bathed in moonlight, its pale glow illuminating a path stretching into the distance. The sky is deep and vast, dominated by an oversized full moon – an enigmatic presence that suggests illusion and mystery.

Below, a quiet town lies in eerie stillness, as if caught between waking and dreaming. Shadows play along the buildings, their elongated forms distorting reality.

A group of animals – dogs or wolves? – stand in the foreground, howling at the moon. They symbolize the duality of human nature: the tamed and the untamed, instinct versus reason.

A road stretches beyond the town into the unknown. Here is the journey through uncertainty, where logic cannot always be trusted, and only intuition can guide the way.

Traditional meaning

The realm of illusion and the subconscious, a space where things are not always as they appear. Deception, confusion, and hidden truths – all are urging us to look beyond surface appearances.

The Moon is also a card of intuition, calling us to trust our inner wisdom when navigating the unknown.

Historically, the moon has been linked to cycles, madness (the word *lunacy* comes from luna, Latin for *moon*), and the shifting tides of human emotions. This card signals that transformation is underway, but clarity is still distant.

Modern interpretation

In the modern world, The Moon reflects the challenge of discerning truth from illusion, a struggle perfectly captured by the rise of AI-generated 'deepfakes.' This technology creates convincing but entirely false realities, preying on our fears and anxieties and embodying the card's themes of misinformation and media distortion.

In such an uncertain landscape, The Moon teaches us that we must look beyond the surface. It urges us to trust our intuition and imagination as powerful tools for navigation. By embracing the unknown rather than resisting it, we allow our deepest insights to emerge from the shadows and guide us toward clarity.

Reversed

Illusions are being lifted, revealing truths previously obscured. Confusion begins to dissipate, allowing clarity and understanding.

Alternatively, this reversal can warn of persistent deception – whether self-imposed or external. It urges caution, particularly in situations where trust is uncertain.

> "All that we see or seem is but a dream within a dream."
> – Edgar Allan Poe, *A Dream Within a Dream*
>
> Poe captures the Moon's essence of illusion and uncertainty, where the line between fantasy and reality becomes beautifully blurred.

The Moon and Folklore

Many cultures have associated the moon with transformation and mystery, often tying it to cycles of change and supernatural forces.

In European mythology, the full moon was believed to awaken the beast within, leading to the legend of werewolves – humans who were cursed to shift into wolves under its eerie glow.

This reflects the Moon's theme of uncontrollable instincts, hidden fears, and the struggle between reason and primal nature.

In Japanese lore, Tsukuyomi, the moon god, was a figure of both beauty and deception. Unlike his sister Amaterasu, the radiant sun goddess, Tsukuyomi was cast into exile after an act of violence, embodying the moon's association with the unknown and the misunderstood. His story parallels the Moon's lesson that reality is often shaped by perception, and that truth is elusive in the half-light of dreams and illusions.

Associations

- *Lunar deities such as Artemis, Selene, and Hecate* symbolize mystery and guidance in darkness.
- *The lunatic* – ancient beliefs linked madness to the full moon, echoing the card's theme of distorted perception.
- *Carl Jung's shadow self* – the hidden, often repressed aspects of our psyche, which the Moon invites us to communicate with and explore.
- *The surrealist movement* – artists such as Salvador Dali embraced the subconscious, much like the Moon card calls us into dreamlike realms.

Final thought

The Moon reminds us that not everything is as it seems, and sometimes, the greatest truths are hidden beneath the surface.

It teaches us to navigate uncertainty with trust in our own instincts.

Though the path ahead may be unclear, the Moon reassures us that in time, the fog will lift, and clarity will come.

19. THE SUN

Positivity, success, the illuminating power of truth, and boundless potential

Keywords

Joy, vitality, success, clarity, confidence, enlightenment, optimism, energy, truth, celebration.

Practical guidance

- *Triumph and illumination.*
- *Things fall into place* – clarity emerges, and confidence fuels your journey forward.
- *Embrace positivity* and celebrate your achievements.
- *Appreciate your success*, and recognize the light you bring to the world.
- *Be bold in your pursuits* and trust that the universe supports your growth.
- *Express yourself freely*, and let joy be your guide.

In many ancient civilizations, the Sun was revered as the ultimate source of life and enlightenment. The Egyptians worshipped Ra, the giver of light, while the Aztecs honored Tonatiuh, believing that the Sun provided strength and vitality.

Imagery and symbolism

A golden sun with a human face gazes down, emanating rays of warmth and vitality. Two children, twins, representing innocence, truth, and the purity of spirit, play together in harmony, reinforcing themes of joy, unity, and enlightenment.

The sunflowers surrounding them are symbols of vitality and personal growth, turning towards the sun in a perpetual quest for light.

The engraved stone wall beneath them reminds us of stability and longevity, anchoring their carefree exuberance in the physical world.

Traditional meaning

This is one of the most positive cards in the Tarot. Success, happiness, and enlightenment. A time of clarity and truth. Everything is illuminated, confusion is dispelled.

This is a time to have confidence in yourself; trust in the universe, and enjoy a period of personal growth.

Just as the sun nourishes life, this card encourages embracing one's potential. Shine brightly in the world.

Modern interpretation

Think about the first images released from the James Webb Space Telescope.

For decades, our view of the cosmic dawn – the birth of the very first stars and galaxies– was shrouded in mystery, and impenetrable clouds of cosmic dust. We knew a fundamental truth was hidden there, but we could not see it.

When the first images from the JWST were released in July 2022, they triggered a global celebration. Pictures like the Cosmic Cliffs of the Carina Nebula were a burst of glorious, undeniable truth, cutting through the darkness and revealing the universe with a level of detail never before seen. It was a true moment of enlightenment. In a time of global uncertainty, the JWST provided a shared moment of pure joy and optimism, perfectly embodying the Sun's power – it illuminates what was hidden, and fills us with wonder.

The Sun in 'The Little Prince'

In *The Little Prince* by Antoine de Saint-Exupéry, the Sun represents comfort and perspective. On his tiny asteroid, the prince watches sunsets to soothe his loneliness, while on Earth, he realizes the Sun shines for all.

This echoes the Sun card's message: illumination, truth, and joy are always available, but one must embrace them. True happiness isn't about controlling the light – it's about opening oneself to its guidance.

Reversed

Temporary setbacks, self-doubt, or a period of diminished clarity. Shadows may cloud your perception, making it difficult to see the path ahead. You may need to actively reconnect with joy and optimism. Be mindful of arrogance or overconfidence blinding you to reality.

> ### The Sun King – Louis XIV
>
> Few figures embody the radiance of the Sun like Louis XIV of France, known as *Le Roi Soleil* – the Sun King.
>
> His 72-year reign brought France cultural dominance, military power, and the splendor of Versailles, where he ruled with absolute authority.
>
> The Sun was his emblem, symbolizing divine right and unwavering control. Yet, his unchecked grandeur led to economic strain and foreshadowed the French Revolution.
>
> The Sun card reflects both the brilliance of success and the burden of great power.

Associations

- *Apollo*, the Greek god of the Sun, music, and prophecy – whose light brings wisdom and vitality.
- *The alchemical Sun* represents gold, the highest achievement in the Great Work.
- In philosophy, the Sun is associated with the concept of illumination and knowledge, as seen in Plato's *Allegory of the Cave*, where the Sun represents ultimate truth.

Final thought

After every dark night, the dawn inevitably arrives. The Sun is a symbol of hope, joy, and renewal, confirming that even in difficult times, light will break through.

The Sun calls on you to embrace your inner radiance, trust in your path, and move forward with confidence. Celebrate your victories, big and small, and know that you are supported.

20. JUDGEMENT

Transformation, spiritual awakenings, and the integration of past lessons

Keywords

Awakening, reckoning, transformation, renewal, higher calling, truth, spiritual evolution, atonement, clarity, rebirth.

Practical guidance

- *Judgement represents a call to action,* urging you to embrace transformation and step into your higher purpose.
- *A moment of awakening,* where past choices and experiences culminate in newfound clarity.
- *Reflect on past actions* with a willingness to forgive both yourself and others.
- *An opportunity for rebirth is at hand.* Embrace it with courage and openness.
- *Redefine your future* by learning from the past.
- *Take responsibility for your choices* and rise to the occasion. Growth comes from self-awareness.

> The Last Judgment, as depicted in Renaissance art, symbolizes humanity's final reckoning and the triumph of divine justice over deception and illusion.

> "Tell me, what is it you plan to do with your one wild and precious life?"
> – Mary Oliver, <u>The Summer Day</u>

Imagery and symbolism

A radiant angel descends from the heavens, trumpet in hand, heralding a moment of profound transformation. Below, three figures – two women, one man – stand amid crumbled ruins, holding hands as they embrace the call of destiny.

Their expressions reflect recognition, reunion, and understanding, suggesting both personal and collective revelation. The remnants of ancient structures hint at the destruction of old beliefs, making way for resurrection, renewal and truth.

Traditional meaning

Awakening and reckoning; the end of one phase and the beginning of another. Past actions have shaped the present, and now is the time for clarity, redemption, and renewal.

This card calls for an honest self-examination and a commitment to transformation. This is potentially a time of enlightenment and spiritual evolution.

Modern interpretation

Judgement speaks of a profound personal awakening, a reckoning that reshapes one's path.

The modern recovery movement, like Alcoholics Anonymous, is a powerful example of this card in action. It is a choice to heed a higher calling, involving an honest reckoning with the past and a release of old burdens.

This process is a true rebirth, embracing second chances and a future of renewed purpose. Judgement affirms the movement's core truth: the past does not define you; your courageous choice to awaken and act today does.

> **In *The Shawshank Redemption*, Andy Dufresne's escape symbolizes Judgement's themes – leaving behind the past, enduring trials, and stepping into a new life of freedom and renewal. His crawl through the sewer pipe and emergence into the cleansing rain is a powerful visual metaphor for a spiritual rebirth, the very essence of the card.**

Reversed

Resisting a necessary awakening out of fear, self-doubt, or an unwillingness to release the past. The refusal to hear a higher calling, leading to stagnation and missed opportunities.

The final years of the Romanov dynasty in Russia serve as a powerful historical example. Faced with a collective call for reform, Tsar Nicholas II instead clung to outdated autocratic traditions. The chance for a peaceful renewal was lost, leading instead to a catastrophic and violent collapse.

Failing to answer the call of awakening often leads to repeating old and destructive patterns.

Joan of Arc embodies the Judgement card's call to a higher purpose. As a young peasant girl, she received a divine calling – a personal blast from the angel's trumpet – urging her to lead an army and reshape the destiny of her nation.

Answering this call was her moment of awakening, a bold choice that required her to release her past life and step into a new, transformative role. Her story is a powerful reminder of the courage it takes to heed the call of destiny.

Associations

- The weighing of souls in Egyptian mythology, where *Anubis judges the hearts of the dead*.
- *The Day of the Dead celebrations*, honoring ancestors and embracing the cycle of renewal.
- The concept of *karma* in Hindu and Buddhist traditions, where actions shape future rebirths.
- In *the Nuremberg Trials*, historical accountability was brought to the forefront.
- In Dante's *Divine Comedy*, souls are judged and guided toward redemption or reckoning.

> "But that is the beginning of a new story – the story of the gradual renewal of a man, the story of his gradual regeneration, of his passing from one world into another…"
>
> – Fyodor Dostoevsky, <u>Crime and Punishment</u>

This final line from the novel perfectly captures Judgement's promise of renewal and rebirth after a long and difficult period of reckoning.

Final thought

Judgement is a call to awaken to your highest potential. It reminds us that transformation is always within reach, and by embracing truth, we liberate ourselves from the constraints of the past. This card affirms that every choice, every action, and every realization brings us closer to enlightenment. Trust in the process of renewal and step forward without fear.

THE WORLD

*Completion, achievement,
and the culmination of spiritual growth.*

Keywords

Completion, fulfillment, harmony, integration, accomplishment, wholeness, unity, journey's end, success.

Practical guidance

- *Celebrate success.* Acknowledge your achievements, both big and small. Reflect on your journey.
- *Seek balance.* Strive for harmony in all areas of your life, integrating the lessons you've learned.
- *Embrace closure.* Tie up loose ends to move forward with clarity. Endings lead to new beginnings.
- *Connect.* Recognize the interconnectedness of all things and your role within it.
- *Stay open.* Remain open to new opportunities and experiences. Every ending is a doorway to a new beginning.
- *Reflect on your journey.* Take stock of your growth and resilience to navigate your next adventure.

> "The greatest thing in this world is not so much where we stand as in what direction we are moving."
> – Goethe

Nietzsche's Eternal Recurrence

Friedrich Nietzsche's concept of eternal recurrence asks us to imagine reliving our lives infinitely, repeating every action and choice. This philosophical idea mirrors The World's cyclical nature – suggesting that endings and beginnings are part of a continuous loop. The card teaches that fulfillment is not static but an ongoing process, urging us to embrace life's cycles with wisdom and intention.

Imagery & symbolism

Completion and unity. At the center of The World stands a luminous woman draped in flowing silver garments. Poised and confident, she embodies grace and mastery.

> "And the end of all our exploring will be to arrive where we started and know the place for the first time."
> – T.S. Eliot, Four Quartets

Her wands. Held in each hand, they symbolize balanced power over the material and spiritual.

The wreath: A circle of lush foliage and white blossoms signify both completion and the eternal cycles of life.

The celestial beings. Instead of the traditional four figures are two birds on the left side of the wreath and two cherubic figures on the right side. These are the elements, cardinal directions, and the application of universal forces.

The city. Distant towers and intricate architecture reflect human achievements and aspirations. It adds depth to the card, grounding the spiritual in the material world.

The rocky outcrop. Symbolizes strength, resilience, and the solid foundation of the journey.

Traditional meaning

The culmination of a major life cycle, signifying achieved goals and wholeness. Harmony, balance, and connection, inviting reflection on past lessons and embracing limitless possibilities. A time to celebrate completion as a stepping stone to greater journeys, integrating experience and understanding.

Modern interpretation

The World affirms the deep satisfaction of successfully completing a long journey. A modern example is earning a Ph.D., which marks the culmination of years of effort. It represents the successful integration of knowledge and the fulfillment of a major life cycle. The card signifies this sense of wholeness, celebrating an achievement that becomes the foundation for a new journey.

Reversed

Reversed, the World may suggest stagnation or a lack of closure. You might feel stuck, struggling to resolve issues or change. Address what holds you back, seek closure, and trust your ability to complete the journey. Introspection is key, urging you to confront fears before moving forward.

> In *The Truman Show*, Truman Burbank's entire life has been a fabricated reality, controlled within a dome. When he finally reaches the edge of his constructed world, he faces a door leading to the unknown. His choice to step through symbolizes the World's message: completion, enlightenment, and stepping into a new, self-determined existence.

Associations

- *The Ouroboros*, the serpent eating its tail, symbolizing the endless cycle of renewal.
- *The Renaissance*, a period of cultural rebirth and integration of knowledge.
- Abraham Maslow's concept of *self-actualization*, reaching one's full potential.
- *Taoism's belief in balance* and harmony with the universe.
- The Hindu concept of *moksha*, liberation from the cycle of rebirth.
- The conclusion of epics like *The Odyssey*, where the hero returns home transformed.

Final thought

The World celebrates completion and unity, honoring the journey and its lessons. It reminds us that every ending starts a new cycle. Embrace interconnectedness, honor past achievements, and step confidently into the future with clarity and purpose. The World inspires us to find beauty in both completion and renewal, urging continued exploration of life's possibilities.

THE SUIT OF COINS explores the tangible world, asking us to be grounded in the here and now. It governs our work, wealth, and the security we build. This journey is one of practical action – cultivating a craft, building a stable home, and creating an enduring legacy. It reminds us that our greatest abundance is found in what we patiently grow and sustain in the physical realm.

BOOKS, CARDS AND APP

THE SUIT OF CUPS delves into the deep, flowing currents of the heart – the realm of emotion, intuition, relationships, and love. This journey is one of connection, asking us to feel deeply, express our compassion, and honor our intuition. The Cups reveal that our truest fulfillment is found not in logic, but in the bonds we form, the joy we share, and the love that guides us.

ADISTANTMIRROR.COM

THE SUIT OF SWORDS navigates the sharp and invisible realm of the intellect – the world of truth, clarity, conflict, and communication.
This journey is one of mental acuity, challenging us to wield our thoughts with precision and courage.
The double-edged blade of the mind cuts through illusion, but it also demands that we speak with honesty and face difficult realities.

BOOKS, CARDS AND APP

THE SUIT OF WANDS is the domain of pure creation, representing the divine spark of passion, ambition, and willpower. This journey is one of action, calling on us to innovate, take bold risks, and pursue our most ambitious visions with unstoppable energy. The Wands remind us that our greatest power lies in our drive to create and our courage to bring a new idea to life.

ADISTANTMIRROR.COM

www.ingramcontent.com/pod-product-compliance
Lightning Source LLC
Chambersburg PA
CBRC091201070526
44583CB00007B/173